Mike Kelley

It's Me Again Hello God It's Me Again

By

Mike Kelley

PUBLISHED by PARABLES
Earthly Stories with a Heavenly Meaning

Mike Kelley

It's Me Again; Hello God; It's Me Again
Mike Kelley

Published By Parables
February, 2020

All Rights Reserved. No part of this book may be reproduced or utilized in any form or by any means, electronic or mechanical, including photocopying, recording, or by any information storage and retrieval system, without permission in writing from the author.

ISBN 978-1-951497-32-3
Printed in the United States of America

Readers should be aware that Internet Web sites offered as citations and/or sources for further information may have been changed or disappeared between the time this was written and the time it is read.

It's Me Again
Hello God
It's Me Again
By
Mike Kelley

PUBLISHED by PARABLES
Earthly Stories with a Heavenly Meaning

Mike Kelley

Dedication

A sister,

A friend,

And sunshine to all who know her,

Joy

Mike Kelley

Hello God, It's Me Again

 Praying from the Barn this morning

Here the horses kick around

Maybe a mouse or two under the hay

Winds rattle at the doors some

Rain on the roof taping out a tune of sorts

Getting things set for this day

Got a few miles to go

Dark yet before the sun lifts

Seems like a different world in here Lord

You me and a few creatures

My dog Rope just came to visit

Putting a worn saddle on smoke

He is so faithful even in the rain

Going down to the Church house this morning

Then up to the grave place

Will passed, but you know that

He had a bit of a weakness some say

I think it was just the way he was

We swapped pocketknives once in awhile

I looked back over the days I known him

Even back when he was a boy

I remember he got sick on green apples

Then that thing about his woman leaving

He and I join up to serve the country together

Seems so long ago

He got shot and we thought he would not make it then

But I reckon you had other plans

Then we got our picture taken for the newspaper at the Rodeo

Seems he had a way of staying on top them bulls

Me, well not so good

I was with him when he got baptized

His life he really tried to change

Guess we all fall short some

He gave me his whiskey to pour out then

Said he couldn't do it himself

You know he never did take it back on as far as I know

He just couldn't leave a card game alone

They said he had the winning hand when he got shot

The four aces didn't mean much when it cost you your life

The other fellow the sheriff has locked up awaiting the judge

His fate doesn't look none too good I am told

Something about that Judge folks say, Roy Bean

Don't rightly know him myself

Well the point of all this talk Lord is

When you add up the score on Will

Recall he did good most the time

He was my friend

And if you have a rodeo in heaven

He might be the man to put on a bull

In short God, when you make that final judgement

Recall his heart, even when he gambled it wasn't for his own gain

He gave the Widow Clark money to keep her house

Then he paid to get Jimmy Wilson through school

He gave more than his ten percent back to the church

And paid outright for the new bell

He even sat with my dog Rope when he got that bite from the snake

Now it's all in your hands

I will miss him, and I hope you will welcome him

That's my prayer

A-men

Mike Kelley

Hello God, It's Me Again

Sun falling out over the horizon

Day coming to its end

Looking back over it all

Saw men fighting hand to hand

Those men fighting both lost out it seems

The lady they were fighting over got on the train and left them both mad

She took one's watch and the other's money

Maybe when she gets to where she is going you might remind her of the woman at the well

The good part I guess is that the men shook hands after it was all over

There was a man here today giving out bibles to folks, and put some in the town hotel

Folks said he was a Gideon

He didn't charge nothing for them just gave them away

I guess he is like Johnny Appleseed but with bibles

I suppose they both plant something and hope it grows

My dog, Rope got barking at something in the bushes

And when I checked it out it was little Tommy Raymer, he ran away from home

Said he was off to see the world; he was going to be rich

I had one of them there Gideon bibles and gave it to him

Then showed him the story of the prodigal Son

He teared up a bit and went back home, heck it was lunch time anyway

Passed by the sawmill, and there was a man with a wagon load of lumber

It's Me Again, Hello God, It's Me Again

I asked him where he was building

He told me he was helping with a buildup of a church in Blue Creek

Said it should be done come November

I think I'll ride out and visit it on Thanksgiving, says they got a piano

It wasn't long ago we put in some new boards at the home church

Got it painted to

Just doing a bit of housekeeping for you Lord

We don't have a piano but Bert plays gospel on his guitar

Preacher there knows you well like he is family

Getting on to dark now but, I see the woman done lit a candle

Love is burning at the window

It sure feels good to be home

Not a bad day

Mike Kelley

Just sending out my thanks God

A-Men

Hello God, It's Me Again

Snow falling today

That is the way this January will end with a fresh coat of white

Down by the Little Miami the geese don't seem to mind it at all

Then there's a lot of little tracks from the rabbits too

Nature is doing ok it seems here

The waters moving with its happy song

And the Blue Heron is swooping just inches above the flow

The trees hold no leaves, but the squirrels seem not to care

The winds whisper along and echo in the hole at the base of a large Sycamore

There is a fresh clean feel to the air

Life is good here where a campfire heats morning coffee

A good time to realize life that you allow us to celebrate in

I got me my journal and write out my prayers at times

It's more for me to look back in and recall

A book of memories them all, good or bad

Then I see the selfish prayers too

I am ashamed that I would ask for what I don't need

I pray you just overlook those

Lord you are so good in your giving

Taking care of those I pray for

Taking care of me too

It's Me Again, Hello God, It's Me Again

Sometimes I get lost in understanding

When this world is moving in one direction

Then you ask us to not be followers of the world

But, to follow you without question

This thing of faith, wow is it a treasure

I never seen you face to face

But have heard the words you whisper

You gave me a pen at time to spell them out

Print them to a page

I look back at what you had me write

And wonder how it is that you can use the hand of man in this way

I just do as you ask

I have told others that it's with your ink I pray my prayers

And it is, oh I voice them out loud too

I sing some in song

I think of them when looking out over the snow

It's pure, white, and Holy

Today I thank you for a time in this worship

A time to pray

Prayers over the snow

A-Men

Hello God, It's Me Again

Just holding on sometimes trying to find you God

Some got you in their church house they say

Others say the same

Can you be in them all?

Will Christians be of many names?

I read from one bible words

Then another says it different

Did something change when the vale in the temple was torn down?

That day back when Christ was on the cross

What happened to those holy words?

I know your there where-ever I go

Maybe the wrong church yet I hear you whisper

Maybe the wrong bible but I know your teaching

Jesus was baptized in a river

Me I got down in a Kentucky tub

Praise to Jesus, I was changed none the less

Oh, it is so hard to understand this thing called Religion

I believe in you without a name of a church

I believe in you like my Grandpa once told me

He said Boy, Religion is the eyes through which man sees God

It's Me Again, Hello God, It's Me Again

Grandma would read your words and tell me about you when I was little

She had a great vision and it was like she was there

She told me of Jesus at his birth and her face was all aglow

She told of the cross, the whole story, and tears came in a flow

She talked of heaven like she could almost see

She prayed with me in her lap

I may pray with the wrong words

But my heart tells me what to say

That inside part opens up

When out on a horse, or down on my knees

If it be in any Church

Or out in some muddy trail

It may be in the morning early before the sun

And it seems words get lifted all day long

Seems man has you on some timetable

Got you only on a Sunday calendar

Got you only on a hours' time and then rush away

If you are talking and folks leave before you get everything said

Can they hear you over the chicken, taters, and biscuits on the table?

This was all so simple when I was little

I'll take the small doses of religion

And just think about it longer

Pray for understanding

And try to always be your sidekick

I have this dog called rope

It's Me Again, Hello God, It's Me Again

He tags along without question

Maybe I should do the same

I am not asking for anything

Just searching a bit harder

From the saddle seat

Down to the dirt on my boot

Got a lot to think about

A-Men

Mike Kelley

Hello God, It's Me Again

This prayer is one of the memories

It is for a lost friend that has gone on

We were so close, so much in tune with each other

In the sunset of the day when the twilight comes

There is a moment when I can almost hear that voice

I feel the warmth of laughter

The exchange of words and emotions shared

This world held for a while such a lovely soul

Now Lord you do

I have an empty spot in my heart

When I ride out alone, I sometimes cry

Yet I am happy to

Happy that another angel has reached your door

Happy that this earth can't hold back that light

In darkness, I find myself looking to the horizons above

Somewhere I feel a closeness with the stars

Somewhere I know that one that twinkles the most

Is the one so chosen for my lost friend

Thank you, God, for the time we had

It is a treasure beyond measure

We rode the world together

And someday we will ride again

Thank you for that memory

And forgive my tear of weakness

There is one less in the Rodeo here on earth

But oh, what a bell ringing ride it must be in heaven

Thanks for allowing two lives to touch

A-Men

Mike Kelley

Hello God, It's Me Again

Moving down the trail today I found a smile

It was a small bird lifting to the winds

I looked back where it came from and saw a nest

It was empty hanging in the bushes

The last to leave the homestead of birds I guess

It seemed to know where it was going

Or maybe it was like me

Just wanting to see what was around the bend

Maybe something over the next hill

Life was calling to me that way

It was the adventure that called me

I was Like Huck Finn and Tom Sawyer on a horse

It wasn't any river water, but a dusty trail across the land

I've seen some beautiful sights

Those sunrises over the Grand Tetons

Stars in the desert nights sky

Have seen horses running wild with a wish to stay so

Found friends of all colors and races too

I hope that little bird finds its adventure too

Then Lord keep it safe from the harms of life

Give it a purpose in its flight

We have harm ourselves, wars and battles and such

These in my life you have allowed me to overcome

Hold that little bird in soft winds, and happiness

Give it a reason to build a nest of its own

That's my prayer today

One for a sparrow that I know you will watch over

A-Men

Mike Kelley

Hello God, It's Me Again

I am lifting a prayer out of confusion

One that it is in your hands to put to rest

Tears come, and I cannot stop them

I love one, and I love another, both family

Both are parted by dark anger

Maybe words of a picture that is not fully true

Expressions of feelings, not reality

Maybe it is anger over the heart and need for control

Maybe it is something else, that only you know

Even these words I pray may bring down clouds of darkness

I have watched our blood of life be taken too soon

It leaves in its wake anger too deep

Shouts of anger grow into hate

Hate grows into separations

We are not alone in this; the world pushes a wedge between love

We look back to the days before, when all was well

Where did it falter

Who can say that it is well with my soul?

Who can recall those hands that once embraced?

I am a simple old man

Things of such are far beyond me

Looking into the eyes of my horse, or dog

There is a clear understanding

Yet looking into the eyes of my own blood

It is hidden what is held back

If your creatures can know

Then why not people?

Secrets, are not part of the animal kingdom

Why so then, mankind?

I lift this prayer of confusion an outsider lost

Asking not for me but others

To find the door, or window you offer

Before the time of this life slips away

Before the answers are at your gates

The trails are to be taken

I pray they are

As for me, I am a thankful one

A parodical once myself

Lost and drifting

Mike Kelley

My saddle is ready, and the dog is kicking up dust

And if I die before this day ends, I will have said

It is well with my soul

I may be confused about many things

Things between this horizon and yours however, I know

Forgive us our trespasses

And let us forgive others

Lead us beyond temptation

And deliver us home

That's my prayer

A-men

Hello God, It's Me Again

It is a cold January morning today

The air holds wisps of snow

It is cold also in a memory

Today is the day to recall that memory

It was a dream he spoke of

He a man of your word

He a man of dedication

He of whom I lift this prayer

Now gone from this earth

Yet his spirit remains

A man who called out for peace

A man who opened a door from earth to heaven

A vision of what could be

A vision of what should be

We are all of you God

Each of us all

From all that is given life by you

Yet walls are built

A separation between

A division of one over the other

This needs not to be

This was his dream

To break down that division

To see the heart and minds

To see the peace

To see what you gave

It's Me Again, Hello God, It's Me Again

The world wasn't ready for him

Now heaven holds that spirit

Yet here below we hold to those words he spoke

A man directed by you

This is the memory we recall

The memory no cold January day can hold back

The snow that speckles the horizon is as pure as his word

It sparkles in the light as dawn arrives

My prayer is for his mission

My prayer of thanks for his word

My prayer for us also to heed words with understanding

Some will bend a knee and lift a prayer this day

Some will thank you for what was in the man

Some will work for the power beyond the words

Let us be at peace on earth

Let us find you as brothers and sisters

All United

United in your service

This is my prayer today Lord

A-Men

Hello God, it's me again

Praying with a damp tear tonight

Got a letter from my dear brother

He is not doing so well down in his health

His wife too

It was a warm letter to my heart

He polished up some old memories

Thoughts of the back-home days

Back to our youth

Simple things he misses

Same things I miss too

You know Lord how it was

Mom's home cooking

She could take nothing and make it wonderful

Then how our Father showed his care too

He talked of treehouses

I guess kids don't build them anymore

It was the days of summer we loved

But I recall the fun in snows too

Seems we both miss the same things

The good book says words I recall

To put away the childish things when you grow old

Yet it is the memories we cherish

It is something invisible I carry in my saddlebag

Something to take out when you're lonely

Something to bring a smile when recalled

I sure wish the trails that hold us apart were closer

To shake his hand again

To sit and talk with him and his wife

To laugh together one more time

We are growing old and that brings us trials

Mountains we wish to climb

I've been up so many rough sides of those mountains

Traveled too far from home

Now it is such we got to realize the treasure we hold

That one of a touch with our thoughts

Can you warm their hearts with my love God?

Let me have a speck of space

Give them a smile from me

He, my brother is an artist Lord

His hands hold the colors of dreams

She, his wife has been with him

A helpmate just as you brought them together to be

Bless them both with your goodness

If any there be you got for me Lord

Pass it on to them

I will make it through, but oh they could use some extra

Hold them in your hands

And let me hold them in my heart

That's my Prayer

Thanks God

A-men

Hello God, It's Me Again

Today came news that holds me in thought and prayer

You know my sidekick in this life is so private

She keeps her issues to herself

Her health has been like a half broke horse

Never settled in

She was sick yesterday, will be today, and again into tomorrows to be

There is a surgeon that soon will cut into her again

The purpose is to give her a better quality of life

For this, I lift my prayer

Before the calendar turns another month, a few organs will be removed from her in this course

The use of them have failed her and now cause reason to cast them aside

Brave as she is Lord, I know she could use a healing hand in the days ahead.

A fighter of this disease of no cure known to man

The broken body has not dampened her spirt of life

This woman who has held to me in the storms of life is a blessing to me everyday

Hold her in your hands and help her through these days yet ahead

I am praying for her this darken night with a hope you will allow some peace and wellness to be for she

Her eyes are November Brown Lord, as beautiful as diamonds to me

They have seen too many troubles however, and tears

Keep the sparkle dancing there as in her youth

You know her heart, and her mind are of good, bless the other parts that give her purpose and grit

I share this with you with faith that your hand will be used to direct these dealings

Hold me to her with all we can hook together to get her on the other of this mountain

She will never ask for favors, for special treatment, or for anything more than love, I'll be pushing that on myside of the horizons and asking for a helping to be bestowed from yours.

Forgive me for being bold in these requests, in my life you have given me far too many treasures, but this one, this woman, this my wife, my best friend, and sidekick on the trails, well you know her and because you do I ask take from me to give to her days of goodness ahead.

I can fight off the bad guys, and those that bring us down but she my Lord needs you in the fight ahead

Holding on to the ropes of life with a lasso around heaven's door to pull her through this and into her birthday month with a smile to be on the road of recovery

That's my prayer

Thank God,

A-Men

Hello God, It's Me Again

Sometimes, When the wind blows

When sun bakes

When rain screams

When snow drifts

When Ice pelts

When water floods

When fires burn out of control

When all elements show their powers

That is when I know myself best

It is also when I grow the most

One must be at their lowest to feel lifted up

I have felt the hand of God

Thanks God, Amen

Mike Kelley

Hello God, It's Me Again

Rain Touches Softly

No Thunder

No Lightning

Just rain falling

Tender drops kiss, as waters receive

Sounds of splashes, almost a whisper

This intercourse opens the mind

Breezes move softly

A clean fragrance of nature lifts

Light is cast in reflections

Clouds allow a filtered sun to glow

Trees play, reaching and holding dancing drops

Clouds shift, folding and unfolding

Here, thoughts become of life itself

We like circles to waters

Our little splashes widen

What ripple can we make

Then an answer comes

Ours is to be a part

A circle joined by others

An anointment with life itself

A lesson learned

As rain touches slowly

Mike Kelley

Thanks for the rain Lord

A-Men

Hello God, It's Me Again

Just thinking about

Old Boots

How many miles have they seen?

How many others have fallen by the way?

Old leather today still holds a shine

Worn in time to fit my style of life

Never shy in any weather, mud or snow

Kicking out in early hours, while others slumber

Then on to those hours, past sunset

No place in this world are they unwelcome where I travel

Even in God's house, they hold me strongly to trails ahead

They fit well to the pastures and farmlands, over hills, and onto horses as we move together

At days end they have served me well

It's Me Again, Hello God, It's Me Again

Standing by my bed awaiting another mile, on another day

 Thanks for my Boots

A-Men

Mike Kelley

Hello God, It's Me Again

Feeling something with you

The Fog came today

Lightly laying over waters

Calling me to listen

To listen to its prayers

Faint white it waves in breezes

Air cool yet alive and fresh

This is a holy time

A communion with a Greater Spirit

Not a word do I speak

Yet my heart is heard

Moving waters sing within nature

It is a music softly falling over rocks

As fog dances it spreads its wings

Lifting away to the mornings sun

Rays of bright yellow melt away the pure white fog

Then all of nature comes to call

To send a goodbye as horizons clear

Azure blue skies open with Monarch Butterflies

Then comes a robin and a hare

They join by water's edge where fog was

A spirit remains in cool grasses

I have been changed inside

Something pure has come to be

I wish to come again

Come and find the peace within

Peace from a morning fog

Thanks, God for the moment A-Men

Hello God, It's Me Again

A morning of thanks

It is a silver morning sunrise

A mist cool lifts like in prayer

Freshness awakens the senses

Old leather boots leave prints in soft soil

Fog hovers in a faint glow over Watchman's mountain

Cottontails scamper down to bottoms creek

Leafless trees reach upholding limbs extended to horizons of dawn

Rain of the evening awakens the aroma of fall

Whip-poor-wills sound out a lonesome song

It is here that my path follows along behind the old church house

The rusty gate squeaks at its opening

Stones with marks hold the history of these hills

Those that lived and died

Lives that touched others now forgotten

All except one

It is here I lay just a small pine limb

She loved the freshness of its scent

It was Christmas all year to her

Pine combs set above the kitchen window

How she could dream

It was on our silver mornings we would sit

Coffee in a mug and she with a cup of tea

All those dreams unfolded in those moments

Life is like that you know

Dreams are wishes just almost in reach

How her eyes would light up with excitement

Her teacup now sits alone in the cupboard

It's Me Again. Hello God. It's Me Again

Her dreams have passed

I come here to feel her spirit

To whisper words over her stone

Part of her may have left this earth

Yet part will always remain

That part within

The world will never know

What joy I have in this silver morning sunrise

Thanks God

A-Men

Mike Kelley

It's Me Again. Hello God. It's Me Again

Hello God, It's me again

It is a sad darkens that falls

This old world finds yet more to pray about

Tears rain down from faces, looking for answers

To the night we light our candles

Lifting thoughts with words to a Greater Spirit

Hands shake, in the shadow of fear

Fear not for themselves, but others

Those that are fallen, without reason

Across our globe they fall

A world out of control

Tomorrows sun will lift again

Yet, mankind will remember

Mike Kelley

Arms will fold around loved ones

Holding to the love within

We are here for a purpose, everyone

This earth is not our destiny

It will be found beyond

Beyond the sunrises, and sunsets

Beyond the tears

Beyond the sadness of today

When we are called, we leave the dust behind

Our boots lay empty

Yet our feet will walk a higher ground

I will not allow this sadness, to take control

My candle burns its light even in the wind

My heart is given in faith

There within is hope, love, and answers

This world cannot take that away

No matter how evil, may be found in this life

There is goodness yet to find

Goodness to share

Thanks for the goodness

A-Men

It was there that the sun moved behind clouds as just a faint shadow of the cross remained. It was there he was to die as winds moved and a chill filled that upper hill. Winds carried the evil event as the sky darken and the ground shook. He was held in place by steel that tore at the bone and his blood came forth. Then his shadow was no more. It was lifted from the earth in his last words beyond.

Today I look to the shadow of the cross and feel it touch my soul within. It can only be seen if you believe in him as he is. No longer an image, but always the shadow remains within my heart.

Now, these many years later I feel the cold shadow of that cross that on this spring day we celebrate his return. Springtime the time when life renews is fitting as our lives are renewed by the death of the body and the return of his spirit.

Hello God, it's me again

I am awake before in the shadows of the night leaves and the day arrives

It is here I feel close as my mind finds that shadow of the cross

The bells of Sunday will ring today

A call to remembrance

Your houses will fill with those that worship maybe just this one day

This day I lift my prayer not with a shine on my boots

No tie or white shirt do I even own

This is what others see as the costume of worship

Heck Lord you know me the man with holes in his pockets

I don't fit in refinery

I do however wrap myself with respect and worship as I am

This Easter I find myself praying a prayer of thanks for all that was given in the shadow of the cross

I was not there when he was nailed

Nor when they placed him in the tomb

But I am here today sending up my words that this old world could not hold the Savior of mankind

I am here giving thanks for the shadow.

A-Men

Hello God, It's Me Again

Momma cried in her bible

Tears of life to God

The lines marked with stains

As in life she felt its pain

But I never saw Momma cry

Her pages had words she wrote

Just a reminder to herself

A reminder underlined with a tear

Its memory wrinkled to the page

But I never saw Momma cry

It must have been some special time

When it was just her heart and God

The pages held the weight of loss

As she prayed for brighter days

But I never saw Momma cry

Oh, the chapters she read them all

And left a trail behind

Her fingers moved across each line

Each word opened her eyes

But I never saw Momma cry

I lifted a prayer

For the golden gifts within

The wrinkled pages are treasures to me

Each one had a volume to say

But I never saw Momma cry

It's Me Again, Hello God, It's Me Again

Now she's has gone beyond

To a place she needs to be

And know she found her way

Her eyes will sparkle from beyond

And no tear will Momma cry

For those who remain to be

Will turn and find as did she

The path from page to page

And answers from a holy book

And pray never to see Momma cry

Now from a bended knee

Lift words to that heavenly place

To find a smile of peace within

Mike Kelley

Asking the pain of earth to erase

And pray never to see Momma cry

A-Men

Hello God, it's me again

Tonight, the winds blew a welcome breeze
I am reaching out for your help
Not for myself
But one of my blood
Strange is the connection we share
A connection she doesn't really know
One of mystery and love
One of the tired feet in hot boots
A soul that drifted without a horse or saddle
A tumbleweed blowing in the winds of life
Yet, maybe now found reaching out
I have never met her face to face in this life
Yet I do know her
I know her better than she may understand
But you do Lord
Hold her in your hands and keep her
No, we have never met in this life but our shadows have
We crossed the same streets
Walked in the same dirt
If never she opens a door to me
I pray a window is open to you

Mike Kelley

This is my pray for Sarah
Thanks, God
A-Men

It's Me Again. Hello God. It's Me Again

Hello God, It's me again

Woke up this morning to fog on the cattails

Looking out to the day I say a momma deer and two young ones

They were sleeping in the thickets

I guess I woke them up coming around the bend

It was a wonderful sight however

Nature always has a treasure it seems

My Dog Rope well he didn't even bark at them

I looked down at him and I swear he was smiling

Old dog is funny like that

Then I found the same smile on my face

It is cool this morning with that mist lifting

Like waking from a dream

Soon the sun will take it away

This fall season is upon us

Soft and mellow season it is

Looking forward to a bite of pumpkin pie soon

It goes well with morning coffee

I just wanted to give a word of thanks for this day

That treasure of living another

I hope to live it right today

That's what I set my goal for

Well paint is ready with the saddle

Rope scratching at the trail so best be moving along

Talk with you more as the day unfolds

Just again thanking you Lord for this beginning

That's it

A-Men

Hello God, it's me again

Sending up the most thank you prayer I got

Sending up my happiest "Yaw-who" within

It amazes me the power within your care

The one that knows the pull of death and life

That once little boy playing cowboy back in Kentucky

He who grew to be a man with views to share

A warrior without a sword
He, my brother

His Getty-up-go finds me in the dust at times

Mike Kelley

But this fight with the Devil has your hand-painted in that battle

He was born with damage to his heart, you knew that

You knew also that he would grow to make a mark in this life

He who looked to your backyard from his telescope

He who smiles with the light of the moon in his eyes

I myself have traveled the world, he has traveled the universe

You planted a seed within that grew with knowledge

It's Me Again. Hello God. It's Me Again

Lessons he shares in his own way
Maybe it a picture to view

Maybe a word of a bird in the tree

Maybe news of the Moons changing faces

He walks a path in your nature
He stops to point out your wonders within

What an inspiration to all that know him

I am thankful you hold him tightly in your hand

Thankful he will ride more trails in this life

Maybe not on a pony and without a cowboy hat like me

But he will serve humanity in whatever course he takes

Well my tears of thanks warm my face

You are my God and My Brothers Guardian

He is my earthly Hero
That little boy on his pony

Thank you, Lord, for my brother
A-men

Hello God, It's me again

It's a special time

A day that is beginning

Or the day ending

That soft time

The time when it is just you and me

I don't even need to say a word

You know my mind

You know also when I stumbled

The fall

Then you allowed me to get up

Dust off

And move on

Mike Kelley

No matter which trail I took

Just that saddle that held me to the horse

That dog running with the wind

It's good for my heart

That my soul is in your hands

Sunrise, Sunset

Someday I am told

Will come to a new horizon

Looking forward to that one

Till then

I'll spend my soft time with you

Thanks, for the beginnings and endings

And the trails in between

A-Men

Hello God, It's Me Again

Just thought we might talk a little

Got this letter from the pony express today

It is a bit worn from its travels

Some of the words are faded a bit

Its Momma's hand to it

She always worries you know

That's the point of my prayer Lord

She is getting along in this life

It has been a bit hard at times

Can you loosen up an angel to look after her a bit?

She lost her tears that fell to the page

Sure, miss her and Dad

I been on too many trails

Too long gone

Miss those others too Lord

My Brothers and Sister

They are good folks but all home folks

Not at all that way with me and a wind to my back

At times I guess I have been the prodigal Son

Chasing dreams just out of my reach

Got not much to show for the years gone

Worn boots, dog missing a few teeth, and a horse

Hope you can guide my hand a bit

To scratch out a letter back

Mom gave me a bible when I left home

It's Me Again. Hello God. It's Me Again

It sure is nice too, Keep it close in the saddle bag

It helps me stay connected to her and you

Maybe it's time to turn around

Get some homestead dust on my boots

Am a bit afraid though

It seems I have little to share

Got no money, heck less than the widows' mite

Got only myself as ragged as I am

Spent all my days looking for that pot of gold

Help me make up my mind on this one

Should I send a letter or me?

That's my prayer,

A-Men

Hello God, It's Me Again

In the early morning

When the sun takes to the eastern skies

One puts on their boots to face the day

It is never always a smooth ride we take

But we saddle up and ride it anyway

Most times we don't even look for tomorrow

Today calls us to be on the ready

We watch for smoke in the horizons

But, pray we don't see any

We may walk in the wet mud at times

Maybe, at others choke in the dust

Winds rip across our path under dark skies

At times snow so deep, travel is hard to make

Ice hangs cold on fences and hands feel its sting

Then at other times it's blue skies with eagles in flight

Cool waters and shade trees

Maybe a kiss for some lovely Valentine

At the end of the day

When the sun falls in the far western skies

You look beyond with thanks

There is something inside that feels complete

It is a peace with self, and that Greater Spirit

You don't measure the good days and bad

The moment you see the candle in the window

And someone waiting within

You know all is well

The end of the day

Thanks, God

A-Men

Mike Kelley

Hello God, It's me Again

I'm resting well here tonight

Dreams lifting me away

I sure would like to see them gates you got there

I bet they are works of art

I wonder sometimes if things are just a bit put on

I would like to see a nice white picket fence with a cute gate

People like to put up walls around things here on this earth

Guess they never heard of Jericho

Oh, and I don't need streets of gold, just ones without potholes is ok

Then if I do somehow make into that promise land

Mike Kelley

Don't give me a mansion, a bunkhouse and a horse will be more me

I would like to see if angels have wings

It would be nice to see one on a horse

Maybe we could ride together through the clouds

Yelp, and at night-time kick up some stardust

Well that just dreams Lord

You must laugh at me at times

But I take you very serious Lord

Now I lay me down to sleep

I pray my soul is worthy to keep

And if I die before I wake

Give someone else a mansion

I take a cabin by some lake,

A-Men

Hello God, It's Me Again

December Dark

Mornings come quietly in the dark

That old sun sleeping in

It is the moon that watches over me

The dim light smiles though light grey clouds

Another long day ahead

Too much to do, too little time

Too little daylight

Another year will soon arrive

And new calendars decorate our walls

Days ahead just numbers now

No notes written on must-do lists

Thoughts drift into this morning's shadows

Thoughts beyond December's Dark

The what-ifs of life haunt me some

Yet, it is I that am the ghost of my own doings

We learn so much from our mistakes

This becomes knowledge I am told

My old boots need a bit of polish to cover the scuffs

My old life to needs a bit of polish to cover my sins

God you know my heart, my thoughts

You really don't mind my scuffed boots

It is where my feet now take me that counts

Not where I have been

I will light a candle in these last fading days

Let the New Year come as it may

It is today I celebrate, riding into the now of life

It's Me Again. Hello God. It's Me Again

These short days of light will pass

As winters breath comes in the frost

My heart thinks of faces

Those I love to see

Maybe it will be

After this December Dark.

A-Men

Mike Kelley

Our Father which art in heaven

        Hello God, It's me again

Hallowed be thy name

        Holy Lord over us all

Thy Kingdom Come

        You join us on these trails

Thy will be done in earth, as it is in heaven

            You call us to ride with you on this earth as do those in heaven

Give us this day our daily bread

Thanks lord we pray over our beans and taters

And forgive us our debts, as we forgive our debtor and we pray forgiveness for stepping on another mans' foot in this life, and we too forget him for scuffing our boot

And lead us not into temptation, but deliver us from evil

Help us stay on the right trail away for the wrong things the devil kicks out, and keeps us close

For thine is the Kingdom, and the power, and the glory forever, A men

It's your range we ride, it is the call of your hand, and we give all goodness of life back to you.

I know today we don't talk none like in the good book, heck Lord you know our hearts none the less. Just give us a moment to lift our words in your direction for without you darn if I know where we would be. I keep my horse ready, maybe an old dog too, but it's your call we are ready to listen up to and now as we head to the bunkhouse it's a prayer of thanks, we send up your way this night   A Men

This book was written in parables, the Cowboy, the dog and horse are to lift your thoughts and maybe open your eyes from the prayer within.

The song to follow I have written and hope it too brings you something from its words.

It's Me Again, It's Me Again

Hello God, It's me again

Sending up another prayer

My heart is in my every word

My soul lifted to you care

Bended knees in the dirt of life

Whispering to your holy ear

Praying for wisdom from beyond

Holding to you always near

It's me again, it's me again

Holding on, it's me again

Hello God, It's me again

Climbing up a mountain high

Reaching for a heavenly home

A kingdom beyond the sky

Sharing with my fellow men

Words of Commandants ten

And Jesus who gave his life

To Wash away our darkest sin

It's me again, It's me again

Holding on, It's me again

      Mike Kelley

It's Me Again. Hello God. It's Me Again

Mike Kelley

www.ingramcontent.com/pod-product-compliance
Lightning Source LLC
Chambersburg PA
CBHW070048230426
43661CB00005B/819